TITANIC Q&A

TITANIC
Q&A

100+
Fascinating
Facts for
Kids

MARY MONTERO

ROCKRIDGE
PRESS

To all the men, women, and children whose lives have been impacted by the *Titanic* disaster

Interior and Cover Designer: Diana Haas
Art Producer: Janice Ackerman
Editor: Laura Bryn Sisson
Production Editor: Andrew Yackira

Cover Photography: Prismatic Pictures/Bridgeman Images; agefotostock: p. 43: Everett Collection; Alamy Stock Photo: p. 6: World History Archive; p. 25: Stephen Barnes/Titanic; p. 27: Credit: Historic Collection; American Press Association: p. 49; Arnold Genthe Photograph Collection (Library of Congress): p. 19; Bridgeman Images: Title Page: Universal History Archive/UIG; p. 14: CSU Archives/Everett Collection; p. 17: The Titanic Collection/UIG; p. 52: Everett Collection; p. 54: The Titanic Collection/UIG; Francis Browne: p. 32; George Grantham Bain Collection (Library of Congress): p. 5, 9, 18, 21, 55, 57, 63; Library of Congress: p.11, 58, 65; NARA: p. 45, 49, 50, 51, 62; Robert John Welch (1859-1936), official photographer for Harland & Wolff: p. 2, 12, 24, 31, 38, 40; White Star Line: p. 37

ISBN: Print 978-1-64739-680-0 | eBook 978-1-64739-418-9
R0

INTRODUCTION

The *Titanic* was the grandest ship of her time, a modern marvel hosting some of the wealthiest people in the world. But after only a few days at sea, the ship sank to the bottom of the Atlantic Ocean and instantly became one of the most famous **maritime** disasters ever.

Even though she has lain in ruins on the ocean floor for more than one hundred years, the *Titanic*'s mystery and tragedy continue to captivate us. As much as this shipwreck has been investigated, there are still things about it that we don't know—and may never know.

Come aboard now to uncover some of the many secrets of this doomed ship . . .

THE SISTER SHIPS

The *Olympic* (left) and the *Titanic*

TRUE OR FALSE?

*There were actually **three** Titanics.*

TRUE AND FALSE.

The **White Star Line** hired Thomas Andrews to design the most luxurious passenger **ocean liner** of all time. But what's better than one awe-inspiring ship? Three ships! And so the idea of the **Sister Ships** was born. One was the RMS Titanic. *The others were the RMS* Olympic *and the RMS* Britannic.

- -

Q Were there other extravagant passenger ships at the time?

A Yes. The White Star Line's biggest competitor was Cunard Line. Cunard had recently built two magnificent ships, the *Lusitania* and the *Mauretania*.

Q What set the White Star Line sister ships apart from Cunard Line's *Lusitania* and *Mauretania*?

A The Cunard ships could sail faster than the sister ships. But the White Star Line sister ships were bigger, so they could fit many special, luxurious features that the Cunard ships didn't have.

STAT: The *Olympic*'s first voyage began on June 14, 1911, nearly **one year** before the *Titanic*'s, due to construction delays and a coal miners' strike.

Q Were the three sister ships identical?

A Close, but not exactly. Although their original building plans were almost the same, the *Olympic* held her **maiden voyage** earlier, which meant that the shipbuilders had time to improve the design for the *Titanic*. For example, the A-**Deck** on the *Titanic* was enclosed by windows to protect passengers and crew members from sea spray.

STAT: Because of improvements made to the *Titanic* after the *Olympic*'s voyages, the *Titanic* wound up being bigger, weighing **46,328 tons** versus the *Olympic*'s **45,324**.

TRUE OR FALSE?

All White Star Line ship names ended in –ic.

TRUE!

Other White Star Line ships included the Oceanic, the Atlantic, and the Adriatic, just to name a few.

- -

Q Did designer Thomas Andrews travel aboard his ships?

A Yes. Thomas Andrews took great pride in his ships. He was on board the maiden voyages of both the *Titanic* and the *Olympic*.

TRUE OR FALSE?

Another one of the Sister Ships sank, too.

UNFORTUNATELY, TRUE.

While the Britannic *was serving as a hospital ship during World War I, she hit an underwater mine. She sank off the coast of Greece.*

- -

Did You Know?

Most interior pictures representing the *Titanic* were actually taken on the *Olympic*, as she survived the longest of the three sister ships.

BUILDING *TITANIC*

The *Titanic* (left) and the *Olympic*, built side-by-side in Belfast

Q How long did it take to build the *Titanic*?

A Three years. The *Titanic* and the *Olympic* were built alongside each other in Belfast, Ireland. The ships were ordered in September 1908, and Harland and Wolff shipbuilders began construction in 1909. The *Titanic* began her maiden voyage in 1912.

STAT: The White Star Line spent **$7.3 million** building the *Titanic*. In today's dollars, that would be more than $200 million!

Q Was the *Titanic* the largest ship ever built?

A As of 1912, the *Olympic* and the *Titanic* were the largest cruise ships ever. This presented some challenges, as there was no existing space big enough to build such huge boats!

The *Titanic's* builders stand under her propellers in Belfast

Q Was the *Titanic* a passenger ship by design?

A While the RMS *Titanic* was created to be a "hotel on the ocean," her main purpose was to transport mail. RMS is short for **Royal Mail Ship**.

STAT: **3,500** sacks of mail were lost when the *Titanic* went down.

Myth:

A construction worker was trapped inside the ship's **hull**.

Truth:

This eerie *Titanic* legend may have come from the story of the *Great Eastern*, a ship launched in 1858. When the *Great Eastern* was eventually taken apart, a man's skeleton was found inside her hull. However, there is no record of this happening on the *Titanic*.

TRUE OR FALSE?

The **rivets** *used during the* Titanic*'s construction may have caused the ship to sink.*

TRUE.

When the sunken Titanic *was discovered, scientists studied 48 of her rivets and found that the shipbuilders had used not only steel rivets, but also iron ones, which are weaker. The iceberg struck a section with iron rivets, which may not have been strong enough to hold the hull together.*

Q Did the White Star Line try to cut corners to save money on the construction of the *Titanic*?

A Though we now know about the weak rivets, when the chairman of the White Star Line, J. Bruce Ismay, was questioned about cost cutting causing safety issues on the boat, he denied it. He said, "No money was spared in her construction."

CONSTRUCTION BY THE NUMBERS

The number of rivets used on the *Titanic*: **3,000,000**

The number of people who helped build the *Titanic*: **3,000**

The number of workers who died from injuries while building the *Titanic*: **8**

The number of horses who carried the *Titanic*'s main **anchor** from the place where it was manufactured: **20**

TITANIC'S SIZE BY THE NUMBERS

Weight: **46,328 tons**

Length: **882 feet, 8 inches**

Height: **60 feet, 6 inches from waterline to Boat Deck**

Width: **92 feet, 6 inches at widest point**

Depth: **59 feet, 5 inches**

Decks: **9**

Watertight Compartments: 16

LAUNCHING THE SHIP

The *Titanic* on the slipway before its launch

TRUE OR FALSE?

The Titanic *became famous only when she sank.*

FALSE.

When the empty hull of the Titanic *was launched for the first time on May 31, 1911 in Belfast, Ireland, more than 100,000 people came to watch. That's nearly a third of the entire population of Belfast! Two rockets were set off to celebrate. A few people even paid for tickets to view her departure from a bandstand!*

Q How was the *Titanic*'s hull moved into water?

A The **slipway** was covered in over an inch of lubricant (slippery stuff like oil) so the ship could "slip" into the water.

STAT: The lubricants on the slipway included **22 tons** of soap, oil, and tallow (fat).

Q Why was the *Titanic* first launched as an empty hull?

A The *Titanic*'s massive frame was built on a ramp called a slipway and then moved to a **wharf** in deep water. It was in the wharf that her insides were filled with the best machinery and furnishings of the time.

The *Titanic* during its fitting-out stage

STAT: Since the *Titanic* didn't have an engine yet, **five** tugboats were needed to pull her to the **fitting-out** wharf.

STAT: The *Titanic's* weight nearly doubled from the time she was launched as an empty hull—weighing **26,000 tons**—to when the fitting-out process was complete, which brought her total weight to **46,328 tons**.

TRUE OR FALSE?

Titanic almost collided with another ship on her maiden voyage.

TRUE.

After tugboats towed the Titanic *out from her Southampton* **berth,** *her engines were turned on. The suction of the* Titanic's *huge propellers was so strong, it snapped the lines securing a smaller boat, the* New York, *which began drifting toward the* Titanic. *The crash was narrowly avoided, and the* Titanic *continued on her way.*

The *Titanic*, launched

A Yes! Before their first trip, ships have **sea trials** to make sure they're safe. The *Titanic*'s sea trials occurred in the Irish Sea less than two weeks before passengers boarded. She passed with flying colors.

STAT: During sea trials, the *Titanic* had to accelerate to full speed and then stop. She traveled almost half a mile in just over **three minutes** before stopping.

The *Titanic* during her sea trials

STAT: One test during sea trials was turning the ship in a full circle. The diameter of the *Titanic*'s turn was **3,850 feet**.

PEOPLE ON BOARD AS THE *TITANIC* CROSSED THE ATLANTIC

1,317	Total passengers
324	First class passengers
284	Second class passengers
709	Third class passengers
107	Children
2 months	Age of the youngest passenger
890	Crew members
1,175 people	Lifeboat capacity
3,547 passengers and crew	Maximum ship capacity

THE SHIP'S CREW

> STAT: 724 of the 890 crew members were from the city of Southampton, England, where the *Titanic* set sail.

Myth:

The *Titanic*'s passage was supposed to be Captain Edward John Smith's last voyage before retirement.

Truth:

This was a popular tale just after the sinking, possibly created by newspaper reporters. However, just days before the ship set sail, the White Star Line said Smith would continue to be the *Titanic*'s commander until a bigger, grander ship was built.

Captain Smith (at right)

Q Who was in charge of the ship when the captain was asleep, dining, or taking breaks?

A Six **lookouts** took shifts watching the waters, seven **officers** took turns overseeing the ship, and six **quartermasters** shared the job of manning the wheel.

TRUE OR FALSE?

All seven officers on board went down with the ship.

FALSE.

Four officers were assigned to lifeboats and survived the sinking.

- -

Q Who else was in charge of the lifeboats?

A The *Titanic* had on board 29 able seamen: people with special training who were in charge of other crew members. On the night of the sinking, they were charged with manning the lifeboats. Eight of the seamen were sent belowdecks to help passengers evacuate and were never seen again.

TRUE OR FALSE?

All crew members were men.

FALSE.

*Of the 890 crew members on board, 23 were women. Most of the women were **stewards**, who helped care for passengers.*

- -

Violet Jessop, steward, pictured later working as a nurse

TRUE OR FALSE?

A crew member survived disasters aboard all three sister ships.

TRUE.

Unbelievably, steward Violet Jessop survived the sinking of the Titanic, *a crash on the* Olympic, *and the sinking of the* Britannic.

Q Which staff member spent the most time with guests on the ship?

A The chief **purser**, Hugh Walter McElroy, was the passengers' right-hand man. He was one of the only crew members who dined with guests on the ship. He was in charge of delivering wireless messages, storing valuables, renting out deck chairs, and taking reports of broken items in passenger rooms.

J. Bruce Ismay

Q Who was the highest-ranking member of the White Star Line aboard the ship?

A J. Bruce Ismay, chairman of the White Star Line. When he hopped into a lifeboat and saved himself, Ismay also became one of the most controversial survivors of the disaster.

STAT: The two youngest crew members were **14 years old** when they died in the sinking. At least one of them had lied about his age to get the job.

THE PASSENGERS

John Jacob Astor

TRUE OR FALSE?

There were dozens of millionaires on board.

TRUE!

There were many very wealthy people on the ship. The richest was Colonel John Jacob Astor, an American businessman.

- -

Myth:

There was a cursed mummy on board that people blamed for the sinking.

Truth:

While aboard the ship, passenger William Stead told a story about a cursed mummy from Egypt. After Stead died in the sinking, listeners of the story recounted the tale to reporters, who published it as fact. There is absolutely no record of a mummy on board.

TRUE OR FALSE?

A survivor of the ship went on to star in a movie about the Titanic *disaster.*

TRUE.

Dorothy Gibson, a singer, model, and movie star, was twenty-two years old and a first class passenger. Just one month after she was rescued, she starred in the first film about the sinking, Saved from the Titanic. *She wore the same clothes in the silent movie that she had worn when she was rescued from the boat.*

Dorothy Gibson

Q Were there any priests on board?

A Yes. There were at least three Roman Catholic priests on board, as well as a Lithuanian priest and a Baptist pastor.

Q How many animals were on board?

A Dozens! Chief Purser McElroy even helped a friend transport a canary on the ship. There were also many pet dogs and chickens, plus uninvited *rats*, aboard the ship!

STAT: **Three** dogs survived the sinking.

TRUE OR FALSE?

All women and children aboard the Titanic *were rescued.*

FALSE.

Many third class women and children died in the sinking. For example, the Goodwin family, an English husband and wife and their six children, were all lost in the disaster. A few first and second class women and children also went down with the ship.

- -

Did You Know?

Milton Hershey, the founder of Hershey's chocolate, bought a ticket to sail on the *Titanic*'s maiden voyage. A business emergency forced him to cross on an earlier ship, likely saving his life.

TRUE OR FALSE?

There were kidnapped children aboard the ship.

TRUE.

A Frenchman boarded the Titanic *with his two young sons, whom he had kidnapped from his ex-wife to bring to America. The father, Michel Navratil, went down with the ship, but fortunately the boys were rescued. Their mother only discovered where they were when she saw their photograph in the newspaper.*

The Navratil children

FIRST STOPS

Q Where did the *Titanic* begin her journey?

A The *Titanic*'s main **port** was in Southampton, England, where 922 passengers boarded. The *Titanic* departed Southampton at noon on April 10, 1912.

Did You Know?

Four would-be *Titanic* crew members did not get on the ship in Southampton because a slowly passing train blocked their way. Talk about luck!

Q Where else did the *Titanic* pick up passengers?

A The *Titanic* made two more stops before setting course for New York City. Her first stop, around 7 p.m. on April 10, was Cherbourg, France, where 274 passengers boarded. She left Cherbourg two hours later and arrived in Queenstown, Ireland, (now known as Cobh, Ireland) by noon the next day. In Ireland, 123 more people boarded, all second and third class passengers.

Q Did any crew members depart the *Titanic* after Southampton?

A Yes. John Coffey was a young **stoker** who left the ship when she stopped in Queenstown by hiding in a mail sack being carried off the ship! Later, he claimed that he bailed because he had a strange feeling that a disaster was about to strike.

Q Did any passengers get off the ship in Cherbourg or Queenstown?

A In total, 31 fortunate people left the ship in Cherbourg or Queenstown, and seven more got off in Ireland. Father Francis Browne, a Catholic priest, was one passenger who disembarked in Queenstown, even though he was offered free passage to New York by a first class couple. Browne later became famous for his photographs of life aboard the *Titanic*.

Q Did the ship dock in Cherbourg and Queenstown?

A No. She was much too large to dock at either port. Smaller ships brought passengers and mail to and from shore. The SS *Nomadic* was one of these **tender ships** that carried passengers to the *Titanic*. Today she is docked in Belfast, serving as a museum, and is the White Star Line's last remaining ship.

INSIDE THE SHIP OF DREAMS

First Class

First class cabin on the *Titanic*

Q What was the most luxurious way to travel aboard the *Titanic*?

A For the richest of the rich, the *Titanic* had four parlor suites. Two of these were called Promenade Suites because they each had a private 50-foot Promenade Deck, as well as two bedrooms, the only private bathrooms on the ship, and a sitting room. What a way to cross the Atlantic!

STAT: A first class cabin on the *Titanic* would cost $3,500 in today's money. The Promenade Suites would cost $100,000 today!

Q Were all the first class staterooms the same?

A No! There were 19 different stateroom designs in first class. The *Titanic* used different eras in history as inspiration for room decor. Some were decorated like they were from the Italian Renaissance, the French Empire, and more!

Second Class

Replica of a second class cabin on the *Titanic*

TRUE OR FALSE?

The second class cabins aboard the Titanic *were similar to first class cabins on other ships.*

TRUE.

Many of the Titanic's *second class cabins were designed to serve as "overflow" first class cabins when more people bought first class tickets than second class.*

Q What did a typical second class stateroom look like?

A Most of the second class staterooms had white walls, wooden furniture, comfortable sofas, and bunk beds. They even had fresh running water, though they had shared bathrooms.

Third Class

Did You Know?

On ships in the early 1900s, **steerage** accommodations were often large, open dormitories filled with many bunks. The *Titanic's* third class accommodations offered a little more privacy than that. The *Titanic* had individual cabins that could house up to 10 third class passengers.

Q Where were the third class cabins located?

A Third class cabins were in the worst part of the ship, deep belowdecks. Third class passengers could hear the loud noise and vibrations from the engine, and they could often feel the sickly sway of the moving boat.

TRUE OR FALSE?

All 708 of the Titanic's *third class passengers shared two bathtubs.*

TRUE!

In the 1910s, it was normal for people to take a bath only once or twice a week. Each third class room did have its own washbasin for passengers to wash their hands and faces.

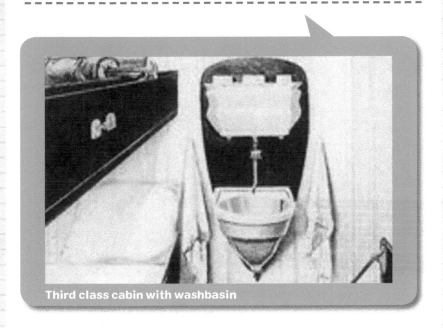

Third class cabin with washbasin

TRUE OR FALSE?

Third class passengers slept on mattresses stuffed with straw.

PROBABLY FALSE.

While other ships provided third class passengers with these scratchy mattresses, most Titanic *beds had real mattresses. Some historians believe that single men slept on straw mattresses with only a blanket, but others say that is a myth.*

CREW QUARTERS

Q Where did the crew sleep?

A Most crew members slept in a dormitory filled with rows and rows of beds. Stewards were the lucky ones: They each shared a two-person cabin with another steward.

Did You Know?

A long corridor called "Scotland Road" ran the length of the ship. Crew members and third class passengers walked this below-deck "road" to get from one end of the ship to another.

Q What were the captain's quarters like?

A There are no known photographs of Captain Smith's home away from home. However, we know that he had a bathroom, a simple bedroom, and a small sitting room—nicer quarters than the other crew members, but less fancy than many of the passengers. When the *Titanic*'s wreck was finally rediscovered, Captain Smith's personal bathtub was still visible!

SAILING IN LUXURY

Drawing of the Turkish Bath aboard the *Titanic*

Q What on earth was the Turkish Bath?

A The Turkish Bath was an unforgettable experience aboard the *Titanic*: a series of hot rooms, followed by "shampooing rooms" for massages, a steam room, and an electric bath. The finale was the "cool room," which was said to be the most ornate and beautiful of them all.

Q Could you get a haircut on the *Titanic*?

A Most definitely! The barbershop was open from 7:00 a.m. to 7:00 p.m.

The *Titanic*'s swimming pool

TRUE OR FALSE?

The swimming pool was only for first class passengers.

TRUE.

Men and women also weren't allowed to swim in the heated, saltwater pool at the same time. At a cost of one shilling per person, women could swim from 10 a.m. to 1 p.m., and men could enjoy from 2 p.m. to 6 p.m.

Did You Know?

The swimming pool on the *Olympic* had two diving boards, but they proved to be a safety hazard, so they were left out of the *Titanic*'s design.

Q What is the most well-known feature of the ship?

A The grand staircase remains the crown jewel of the *Titanic*. A stunning glass dome ceiling allowed sunlight to pour over the wooden staircase. An ornate clock served as the centerpiece.

A similar grand staircase on the *Olympic*

Q Could passengers explore the outdoor decks on the *Titanic*?

A Even though it was chilly, all classes could enjoy the *Titanic*'s outdoor decks. Second class passengers had three open decks, third class passengers could visit the well decks and poop deck, and first class passengers enjoyed the Promenade Deck, which circled all of A-Deck.

THE *TITANIC*'S OPERATIONS

Q How did the ship communicate with other ships or people on land?

A *Titanic* communicated using new wireless telegraph equipment called the Marconi system, named after its inventor, Guglielmo Marconi. They used this equipment to send messages in Morse code.

The Marconi Room on the *Olympic*

Q Where did the wireless operators work?

A The Marconi Room was actually three rooms: the operator's main room, a silent room with radio equipment, and the Marconi operators' bunks.

STAT: Stokers, also known as firemen, kept **29 boilers** fed with coal to keep *Titanic*'s furnaces burning and the engines running.

Q How was the ship steered?

A The *Titanic* had two main wheels: one on the **bridge**, and one in the **wheelhouse**. The wheelhouse was also home to the control panels that lowered the watertight doors.

Q How did the lookouts communicate with the officers?

A The **crow's nest** stood high above the ship, and it had a phone that rang directly to the wheelhouse. The lookouts used the phone to send ice warnings and share any unusual sightings—like the iceberg that doomed the ship.

STAT: The lookouts worked in **two-hour** shifts around the clock. There were always two lookouts on duty.

CURIOUS CARGO ON BOARD

Q What was the most expensive item lost on the *Titanic*?

A According to claims filed by survivors of the ship, the most expensive item lost was a 19th-century oil painting. The owner of the painting, who survived the sinking, claimed that the piece was worth $100,000, equal to over $2 million today.

STAT: Five grand pianos went down with the ship.

TRUE OR FALSE?

One passenger lost his perfume collection when the ship sank.

TRUE.

Adolphe Saalfeld was a first class passenger and perfume maker who had brought 65 vials of perfume on the Titanic *with him. Though Saalfeld survived the sinking, the perfume went down with the ship. Nearly 90 years later, the vials were recovered—and, much to the search team's surprise, they could still smell hints of lavender and rose!*

STAT: The *Titanic* was carrying **twelve cases** of ostrich feathers in its cargo.

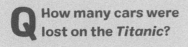

Q How many cars were lost on the *Titanic*?

A Only one: a brand-new, very expensive car belonging to first class passenger William Carter.

TRUE OR FALSE?

The Titanic's *bandleader was found with his violin.*

TRUE.

Sadly, bandleader Wallace Hartley died in the sinking. His body was found floating in the Atlantic 10 days later with his violin case still strapped to his body. Upon its discovery, the violin was returned to his fiancée, Maria. Much later, in 2013, it sold for $1.7 million. It is one of the most treasured artifacts from the sinking.

STAT: Fully loaded with passengers and cargo, the *Titanic* weighed **52,310** tons. Around **6,000** of those tons were from coal used to power the ship.

TRUE OR FALSE?

All of the jewelry that went down with the ship was lost forever.

FALSE.

In fact, many pieces of exquisite jewelry have been discovered during expeditions to the sunken ship. Collections of diamond bracelets, necklaces, and more have been brought to the surface. One explorer even found a bag of gems!

14,000 gallons	Water used daily
75,000 pounds	Fresh meat
40 tons	Potatoes
250 barrels	Flour
10,000 pounds	Sugar
40,000	Eggs
6,000 pounds	Butter
1,000	Loaves of bread
36,000	Apples
1,200	Quarts of ice cream
1,500 gallons	Milk
16,000	Lemons
10,000 pounds	Dried beans and rice
2,200 pounds	Coffee
10,000 pounds	Cereal

DAILY LIFE

À la Carte Restaurant

Q Were meals on the *Titanic* free?

A On other ships, third class passengers had to bring their own food. But on the *Titanic*, food was included with most tickets. Menus changed daily, but passengers couldn't choose what or when they ate. There was also a first class dining room called the À la Carte Restaurant, where diners had to pay more, but could eat at any time.

TRUE OR FALSE?

Passengers were assigned seats in the dining rooms.

TRUE.

Passengers in first and second class were usually grouped with the same people the entire time they were on board.

Q What did first class passengers do to pass the time?

A From the squash courts and gymnasium to the reading and writing room, first class passengers had something to do at any time of day.

Did You Know?

The *Titanic*'s first class gymnasium had a mechanical horse and a mechanical camel, so you could go for a ride in the middle of the Atlantic!

Gymnasium on the *Titanic*

Q How did third class passengers pass the time aboard the ship?

A They played deck games, listened to music played by their fellow steerage passengers, and danced!

Q What happened if people got seasick?

A There were two cures for seasickness at the time: beef broth and smelling salts. Some people were so seasick that they spent much of the voyage resting in their cabin. For the very ill, the *Titanic* had its own passenger and crew hospitals.

TRUE OR FALSE?

Third class passengers could not mingle with first and second class passengers.

TRUE.

All of the classes had separate dining rooms, walking decks, smoking rooms, etc. Most never crossed paths with one another.

- -

Q How did passengers move throughout the ship?

A Passengers moved between decks with elevators, which were called electric lifts at the time. First class had three lifts, and second class had one. First class lifts even had attendants to operate them, and comfortable sofas to lounge on during the journey from deck to deck.

Did You Know?

The White Star Line had custom designs for many everyday items on board—like playing cards, dishes, and matchboxes.

Smoking room aboard the *Titanic*

TRUE OR FALSE?

There were male-only smoking rooms.

TRUE.

The first, second, and third class areas of the ship each had rooms just for men to have an after-dinner smoke and play card games.

Q Where would the women gather?

A Though there weren't any female-only rooms, the first class reading and writing room and reception room were filled mostly with women. They spent their time drinking tea, enjoying live music, and chatting with other passengers.

HITTING THE ICEBERG

TRUE OR FALSE?

Captain Smith ignored ice warnings.

TRUE AND FALSE.

Captain Smith knew they were entering a dangerous ice field, but he changed the ship's course only slightly. The Marconi operators had received seven ice warnings from nearby ships, but two never made it to the captain. Others were given to the lookouts.

- -

Myth:

Captain Smith was trying to beat a speed record.

Truth:

The ship's maximum speed was 23 **knots**, and it was "only" going about 22 knots when the *Titanic* hit the iceberg. There is no known proof that Smith was trying to break any records.

The iceberg believed to have sunk the *Titanic*

TRUE OR FALSE?

The wireless operators told other ships to "shut up" when they sent ice warnings.

TRUE.

Less than an hour before the Titanic struck the iceberg, nearby ship the Californian sent a message that they were stopped in an ice field and wouldn't continue until morning. Busy with his other transmissions and frustrated by the interruption, the Titanic's Marconi operator Jack Phillips responded with a message of "D-D-D," which was **Morse code** for "stop sending messages." The Californian's operator then turned off his radio and went to bed.

Q What happened after the lookouts spotted the ice?

A The lookouts immediately phoned the bridge with the urgent message: "ICEBERG! RIGHT AHEAD!" Sixth Officer James Moody answered and signaled the engine room to stop the engine. He ordered "full astern," which reversed the ship's direction, and then ordered the ship's wheel "hard astarboard," or left, to try to move around the berg.

STAT: It is believed that less than **one minute** passed between the time the lookouts spotted the iceberg and when the Titanic collided with it.

DAMAGE TO THE SHIP

Myth:

The iceberg tore one giant hole in the bottom of the ship.

Truth:

For many years, people believed only a huge gash could have caused the Titanic to sink so quickly. But upon the *Titanic*'s discovery, explorers found evidence suggesting six small gashes in her hull.

Q Why didn't the watertight compartments save her?

A The *Titanic* could stay afloat with four watertight compartments breached. The placement of the six gashes meant water immediately poured into at least five compartments, dooming the ship.

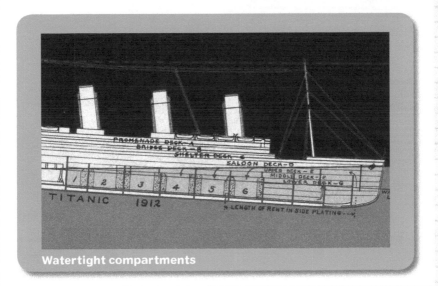

Watertight compartments

TRUE OR FALSE?

If the Titanic's *crew had not reversed the engines and turned the ship when they spotted the berg, the impact would not have been as deadly.*

TRUE.

Most experts believe that if the Titanic *had simply hit the iceberg head-on, there would have been time to evacuate all of the passengers to other ships and* **lifeboats** *before sinking.*

Q Did passengers and crew know something was wrong right away?

A Some passengers saw ice fall onto the decks, and most reported feeling a light jolt. The areas of the ship above the waterline felt very little, but below deck, crew and passengers heard the roar of the collision. Engineers and fire stokers knew there was danger right away when water started pouring into the ship.

Myth:
Titanic had a coal fire burning before the sinking.

Truth:
Ten days before the ship departed, a coal fire began in one of Titanic's coal bunkers. It continued to burn while she was at sea. Some people believe this weakened the bulkheads and caused the ship to sink faster, but most experts disagree.

ABANDON SHIP!

Collapsible lifeboat D

Q How many lifeboats were on the ship?

A Although the original plan was to put 36 lifeboats on the *Titanic*, designers thought the deck would look too cluttered with that many boats. So the *Titanic* left on her maiden voyage with only 20 lifeboats, four of which were collapsible.

Did You Know?

The *Titanic* was scheduled to have a lifeboat drill on the morning of April 14. However, Captain Smith canceled it.

Q How long did it take the crew to start loading lifeboats?

A After impact, the ship's designer, Thomas Andrews, quickly realized that the ship would sink . . . and fast. Within 20 minutes of striking the iceberg, the crew was ordered to ready the lifeboats. The first lifeboat was lowered at 12:45 a.m.

STAT: Passengers and crew had only **two hours and forty minutes** to evacuate the ship between the time it struck the iceberg and the time it slipped beneath the ocean.

Q If there was room for 1,175 people aboard the lifeboats, why were only 712 saved?

A Right up until the *Titanic* actually sank, many passengers believed they were safer aboard the grand ship than in a tiny lifeboat. This meant that many stayed back until it was too late. Some members of the ship's crew were also afraid that filling the lifeboats with too many people would cause the boats to collapse.

STAT: There were only **27 people** aboard the first lifeboat, even though each lifeboat could safely hold between **40** and **65** grown men.

TRUE OR FALSE?

All of the lifeboats were launched.

FALSE.

There simply wasn't enough time, nor enough crew members with proper training, to launch all the boats. Collapsible lifeboats A and B were never properly launched. Instead, when they reached the water, collapsible B overturned, and collapsible A's canvas sides were never raised, allowing water to spill into the boat.

Q How did the *Titanic* call for help while she was sinking?

A The ship's wireless operators worked tirelessly, repeatedly sending distress signals **CQD** and **SOS** to nearby ships. They also set off rockets. Many ships heard the *Titanic*'s call, but none were close enough to make it to her in time.

Myth:
Nearby ship the *Californian* ignored the *Titanic*'s calls for help.

Truth:
The closest known ship, the *Californian*, might have been able to get to *Titanic* in time. However, the ship's radio operator had already gone to bed for the night. Crew members might have seen the *Titanic*'s **distress flares** but not been able to figure out where they were coming from. As soon as they learned of the *Titanic*'s disaster the next morning, they rushed to her.

TRUE OR FALSE?

Only women and children were allowed in the lifeboats.

MOSTLY TRUE.

Under an order from Captain Smith, most officers only allowed women and children aboard the boats. Some officers did allow men to board lifeboats when there were no women and children around to fill the empty seats.

Myth:

More third class passengers died in the sinking than first and second class passengers because they were locked behind gates.

Truth:

More third class passengers *did* die, but probably not because they were trapped. The first and second class staterooms were much closer to the decks, making it easier for those passengers to get to the boats. Many of the third class passengers didn't speak English, which made it difficult for them to understand the situation and to find their way through the winding corridors. Finally, many of the third class passengers were men, which meant that even those who did make it to the decks weren't allowed a seat in most lifeboats.

TRUE OR FALSE?

The musicians played music to calm passengers right up until the ship sank.

TRUE.

The musicians have been hailed as heroes for playing until the very end.

INTO THE WATER

STAT: The water temperature when the *Titanic* sank was **28 degrees Fahrenheit**.

Q Did everyone have a life belt?

A Yes. Although there weren't enough lifeboats to fit all the crew and passengers, most passengers got one of the 3,560 **life belts** on board. Even though they didn't drown, most people who ended up in the freezing water died within 15 to 30 minutes from hypothermia.

Lifebelts of survivors piled on the *Carpathia*

A Collapsible A quickly filled with ice-cold seawater. Only 13 people managed to survive the night in the frigid boat. Lifeboat 14 eventually came back to rescue the survivors, and collapsible A was left to float away with three bodies still inside. Collapsible B was upside down, but about 25 people survived by standing on top of it.

Flooded Collapsible C when found by rescuers

Did You Know?

The lifeboats had tins of biscuits aboard, but the passengers either didn't find them or didn't choose to eat them.

TRUE OR FALSE?

Lifeboats didn't return to rescue swimming passengers for fear that people swamping the boats would sink them.

SOMEWHAT TRUE.

While this was a fear, crew members mostly rowed away out of worry that the suction of the sinking liner would pull them under. Several boats later returned to the site of the sinking, but by that time, most people in the water had already frozen to death.

Lifeboat B recovered after the sinking

Q Why were there so many different memories of what happened when the ship sank?

A Just before the *Titanic* sank, her power went out. That left only the moon to light the ocean, which made it difficult for passengers and crew to see exactly what was going on.

Q Did any of the lifeboats try to row for help?

A Yes! The lights of a ship were visible in the far distance, so it is believed that Captain Smith ordered lifeboat 8 (the first lifeboat to be lowered from the port side) to row for it. They did so, but the distant ship kept moving away. The mystery ship was never identified.

Q What was it like on board the lifeboats?

A It was freezing cold, and many people only had light jackets. Some only wore nightgowns. Others were still in their fancy evening clothes, and some were wrapped in blankets. Some cried, others prayed, and they all searched for a rescue ship.

Artist's drawing of the sinking

TIMELINE OF THE SINKING, APRIL 14–15, 1912

9:00 a.m.   The *Caronia* sends the first of many ice warnings.

9:20 p.m.   Captain Smith goes to bed, with instructions to wake him if conditions get bad.

10:00 p.m.   Lookouts Frederick Fleet and Reginald Lee take over the watch, warned to "keep an eye out for small ice."

10:55 p.m.   The *Californian* sends a warning that they're stopped in an ice field.

11:30 p.m.   Fleet and Lee begin to notice a "haze" right in front of the *Titanic*.

11:40 p.m.   Lookouts spot an iceberg and phone the bridge. Less than a minute later, the iceberg scrapes the side of the ship. Captain Smith is informed that the mail room is flooding and at least five of the watertight compartments have been breached.

12:00 a.m.   The crew is ordered to ready the lifeboats.

12:20 a.m.   The *Carpathia* hears the *Titanic*'s distress call: "Come at once. We have struck a berg. It's a CQD, old man."

12:45 a.m.   The first lifeboat is lowered.

2:15 a.m.   The final distress message is sent from the *Titanic*: "SOS SOS CQD CQD *Titanic*. We are sinking fast. Passengers are being put into boats. *Titanic*."

2:18 a.m.   The *Titanic*'s lights go out.

2:20 a.m.   The *Titanic* plunges into the ocean.

4:10 a.m.   The first lifeboat reaches rescue ship *Carpathia*.

9:00 a.m.   All survivors have been picked up, and the *Carpathia* heads toward New York.

THE *CARPATHIA*

Q How did the *Carpathia* find out the *Titanic* needed help?

A The wireless operator on the *Carpathia* missed the first distress calls from the *Titanic* because he was on the bridge. While he listened to messages before going to bed, he heard the *Titanic*'s call for help. He immediately woke his captain with the unbelievable message that the *Titanic* was in trouble.

The *Titanic*'s distress call

A Yes! Captain Rostron knew how dangerous it was, so he posted extra lookouts as they sped through the ocean to reach *Titanic*. He later said, "I can only conclude another hand than mine was on the helm," meaning he thought God must have guided him through the ice fields.

Did You Know?

To speed up the *Carpathia* and reach the *Titanic* faster, its captain turned off the ship's heat and hot water to send extra steam to the engines. Captain Rostron woke all the stokers to help shovel coal and power the ship.

The *Carpathia*

Q Did the passengers on board *Carpathia* know what was happening?

A Some did. A few noticed that the ship had changed course, and since the heat had been shut off, some noticed when it became colder. Some didn't realize anything was wrong until *Carpathia* was alongside lifeboats and pulling in survivors.

TRUE OR FALSE?

Captain Rostron did not know the Titanic *had sunk until he arrived at the scene.*

TRUE.

Although he knew the Titanic *was in danger, nobody believed the* Titanic *would sink. As they raced to the* Titanic, *Rostron's crew quickly prepared to take on all 2,207 passengers and crew. They arrived at the* Titanic's *last known position by 4 a.m. and were shocked when there was no sign of the ship. Eventually, people on the* Carpathia *spotted a green flare fired by lifeboat 2 and began rescuing survivors from the lifeboats.*

- -

Q How did survivors get from the lifeboats onto the *Carpathia*?

A It was too icy and dangerous for the *Carpathia* to go to each lifeboat, so instead, the *Titanic* survivors rowed to her. One by one, lifeboats arrived at the *Carpathia*'s side, and both the passengers and their lifeboats were carefully lifted up to the ship.

RESCUE ARRIVES

Q What happened when survivors came aboard the *Carpathia*?

A Most *Titanic* survivors had only the clothes on their backs when they arrived on the *Carpathia*. Passengers and crew of the *Carpathia* banded together to help by providing warm food and giving up their beds, clothing, and blankets. They even helped form a survivor relief fund.

Lifeboats approach the *Carpathia*

Q Was the *Carpathia* a luxury ship like the *Titanic*?

A No! In fact, when the *Carpathia* was first launched, it didn't even have first class rooms.

TRUE OR FALSE?

The Carpathia's *original destination was New York City.*

FALSE.

The Carpathia *had actually left New York City on April 11, headed for Europe. Upon picking up the* Titanic's *survivors, Captain Rostron made the difficult decision to return to New York City.*

Survivors aboard the *Carpathia*

TRUE OR FALSE?

Captain Rostron considered taking survivors to Halifax, Canada, instead of New York City.

TRUE.

Halifax was closer, but the path there would have been icy. Rostron and J. Bruce Ismay, the chairman of the White Star Line, decided to take the survivors to New York City.

Q Why was Ismay called a coward?

A On the *Carpathia*, Ismay asked for a room all to himself, when most had to share rooms and sleep on the floor. He kept to himself there. This, along with his survival when so many had died, led the press to call him a coward.

Q What happened to the bodies of the people who froze in the water?

A The ship *Mackay Bennett* was sent to find the bodies, but only discovered some. These were either buried at sea or brought to Halifax for burial. Some bodies were never found.

Did You Know?

Captain Rostron was hailed as a hero for his actions in saving the *Titanic* survivors.

BREAKING NEWS: THE UNSINKABLE SINKS

Q How did the world find out about the *Titanic* disaster?

A Since many ships and some wireless stations on land heard the *Titanic*'s calls for help, word of the disaster spread quickly. Survivors frantically sent telegrams from the *Carpathia* to their loved ones letting them know they were safe. While still on the water, Captain Rostron refused requests from reporters for more information. Eventually, the *Olympic* and White Star Line confirmed the details of the disaster.

TRUE OR FALSE?

Some newspapers reported that everyone had survived the Titanic *disaster.*

TRUE.

At first, a wide variety of news stories ran on front pages. Some told a tale of all passengers and crew members being saved, and others reported that the Titanic *was being towed back to port after hitting an iceberg. It would be days before the real story would come to light.*

SURVIVORS ARRIVE IN NEW YORK

TRUE OR FALSE?

The Carpathia *sailed to the same berth at which the* Titanic *would have arrived.*

TRUE.

When the Carpathia *arrived in New York City on the evening of April 18, 1912, it docked in the White Star Line berth. After dropping off the* Titanic's *used lifeboats, the* Carpathia *went to its own berth, where the passengers disembarked.*

Q Who was waiting for the survivors when they arrived?

A Tens of thousands of people waited on shore! Tugboats full of photographers trailed the *Carpathia* as she made her way into the New York pier. They used megaphones to shout offers for money in exchange for stories.

TRUE OR FALSE?

The crowd cheered when survivors began departing the Carpathia.

FALSE.

Many accounts of the people present in New York tell of a respectful silence that fell over the crowd as the first survivors departed the ship.

Q Who got the first story in print?

A One reporter, Carlos Hurd, was a passenger on the *Carpathia* and had already spent days secretly collecting survivors' stories. When the tugboats came alongside the *Carpathia*, Hurd tossed his notes to his editor so his newspaper could be the first to report the stories.

Newspaper boy selling papers outside the White Star Line office in London

Q Who made up the crowd of people awaiting the survivors?

A Family and friends of *Titanic*'s passengers were anxious to hear of their loved ones' fates. Reporters wanted the first interviews. Doctors, nurses, priests, and the Salvation Army were there to help.

The crowd awaiting Titanic survivors in New York City

SURVIVORS

It's estimated that around 712 people survived the wreck.

	Female Survivors	Male Survivors
First Class	143	58
Second Class	105	13
Third Class	121	60
Crewmembers	20	192

THE INQUIRIES & THE IMPACT

Q Did anyone investigate what caused the sinking?

A There were two major **inquiries** into the sinking. The United States Senate inquiry started the day after the *Carpathia* docked and ended on May 25. The British inquiry began on May 2 and lasted through July 3.

Q Why were there inquiries?

A The inquiries were set up to find out exactly what caused the *Titanic* to sink, why so many lives were lost, and what could have been done differently.

TRUE OR FALSE?

No women were interviewed during the investigation.

FALSE.

Although Margaret Brown was frustrated that investigators would not allow her to tell her side of the story, some women did share their experiences during the inquiries.

Q Who was blamed for the sinking?

A After the inquiries, the Americans placed the blame on Captain Smith, but the British inquiry didn't place the blame on anyone.

The US Senate Inquiry

Q What was done to make sure a tragedy like this would never happen again?

A After the inquiries, all ships were required to have enough lifeboats for everyone on board. Ice patrols kept watch over icy waters and warned ships of dangerous bergs. All ships were also required to have 24-hour radio systems to stay in contact with other ships.

LASTING FAME

Q What happened to survivors after they docked?

A Some went home to Europe. Some shared their stories with the news or during the inquiries. Some crew went back to work on other ships. Many survivors always felt the sadness of having lost loved ones in the sinking.

STAT: The youngest survivor was Millvina Dean, who was just **two months old** when she was brought aboard a lifeboat. The oldest surviving passengers were **64 years old** when the ship went down.

The bow of the wrecked *Titanic*

A The *Titanic* was the biggest news event of 1912, but in all the years that followed, she has never been forgotten. When the ship was discovered on the seafloor in 1985, interest swelled! At the time of her discovery, some survivors of the disaster were still alive and able to share her story. When the movie *Titanic* was released in 1997, an entirely new generation of *Titanic* fanatics was born.

STAT: The 1997 *Titanic* movie used a **5 million gallon** tank for the interior sinking scenes.

Myth:

The *Titanic*'s wreck was discovered as part of a secret military mission.

Truth:

Robert Ballard, whose team found the wreck, used some funding from the US Navy to develop a remotely controlled deep-sea vessel called the *Argo*. The *Argo* carried out secret Navy missions, but Ballard was also allowed to use it to search for the *Titanic* wreck.

GLOSSARY

anchor: a weight to keep a ship in place

berth: a home to ships when they are not sailing

Boat Deck: the topmost deck on the *Titanic*, where lifeboats were stored

bridge: The forward part of the Boat Deck, from which the ship is commanded. The bridge provides a clear view over the front of the ship.

CQD: a distress call used on Marconi wireless radios that meant "All Stations: Distress"

crow's nest: a tall structure that extends above the ship and serves as the lookouts' watch point

deck: A floor on a ship. The *Titanic* had 10 decks. The topmost, the Boat Deck, had areas for promenading, the bridge, and the life-boats. A-Deck, also known as the Promenade Deck, had special entertainment areas for first class passengers. Decks B through F were passenger decks, and decks G and below housed essential machinery like the engine and boiler rooms.

distress flare: a small "rocket" that lets out a shower of bright sparks in the air, showing that a ship needs help

fitting-out: the process of completing the interior of a ship

hull: the main body of a ship, including the bottom, sides, and decks

inquiries: Government investigations. There were both British and American inquiries into the sinking of the *Titanic*.

knots: a speed measure for boats, equal to one nautical mile per hour

life belt: A personal flotation device designed to keep a person afloat in water, also called a life vest. *Titanic*'s life belts were made from cork.

lifeboat: a small boat that can be lowered into the ocean in case of an emergency

lookout: a person whose job is to watch the sea and report any upcoming hazards

maiden voyage: a ship's first trip

Marconi Room: where the *Titanic*'s wireless officers sent and received telegraph messages with people on land and other ships

maritime: relating to the sea

Morse code: a code of dots and dashes used to send messages

ocean liner: a ship that carries passengers across the ocean, also known as a "liner" or "passenger liner"

officer: A person in charge of running the ship. An officer was always present at the bridge.

poop deck: the highest deck in the back of the ship

port: A harbor where ships dock. "Port" can also refer to the left side of a ship ("the port side").

promenade: "To promenade" means "to walk." The Promenade Decks had rooftops and open windows so first class passengers could comfortably walk.

purser: the crew member in charge of money and valuables on board

quartermaster: the crew member who steers the ship

rivets: metal rods used to fasten things together

Royal Mail Ship (RMS): A prefix used to indicate that a ship is carrying mail from England. Other ships used the prefix "SS," which stood for steamship.

sea trials: a series of tests to make sure a ship is ready for travels

Sister Ships: Ships of the same class with a nearly identical design. The three luxury liners the *Olympic*, the *Titanic*, and the *Britannic* were sister ships.

slipway: a ramp used to move boats to and from water

SOS: Morse code signal for help

steerage: the third class compartment, for passengers whose tickets were the least expensive

steward: a crew member in charge of taking care of passengers aboard a ship

stoker: a crew member who keeps the boilers on a steamship powered with coal

tender ship: a boat that transports people and supplies between shore and a larger ship

watertight compartments: parts of a ship that have water-tight doors that can be closed off from the rest of the ship

wharf: a structure for a boat to dock at

wheelhouse: the area of a ship that houses the steering wheel

White Star Line: a British shipping company that transported passengers and cargo between Europe and the United States

RESOURCES

Want to find out more about the *Titanic*? Start here!

SOCIETIES AND MUSEUMS

Premier Exhibitions: *Titanic*: The Artifact Exhibition

SS *Nomadic*, Belfast, United Kingdom

Titanic Belfast, United Kingdom

Titanic cemeteries, Halifax, Nova Scotia

Titanic Historical Society, Indian Orchard, Massachusetts

Titanic International Society, New Jersey

Titanic Museum, Branson, Missouri

Titanic Museum, Pigeon Forge, Tennessee

WEBSITES

Encyclopedia Titanica (Encyclopedia-Titanica.org)

Titanic Facts (TitanicFacts.net)

Titanic Inquiries (TitanicInquiry.org)

Titanic (Titanic-Titanic.com)

BOOKS

DK Eyewitness: Titanic, by Simon Adams

Explore Titanic: *Breathtaking New Pictures, Recreated with Digital Technology*, by Peter Chrisp

I Survived the Sinking of the Titanic, 1912, by Lauren Tarshis

Voices of the Titanic, by Mary Montero

MEDIA

A Night to Remember

National Geographic: Secrets of the Titanic: A Legend Surrenders Her Mysteries

Titanic: The Complete Story (The History Channel)

A NOTE ON SOURCES

When the *Titanic* sailed, records like passenger and crew counts were still kept by hand, without the technology we have today. The confusion that unfolded during the sinking also made knowing exact counts difficult. Official records, including those of the government inquiries, often contradict one another. In this book, I've used the numbers arrived at by Encyclopedia Titanica's analysis and cross-referencing of the multiple and differing sources available.

ACKNOWLEDGMENTS

Thank you to my husband and sweet girls, who endure my daily *Titanic* movie quotes and indulge me in endless *Titanic* teas, dinners, museum visits, and history lessons. To my parents, for showing me the importance of a relentless work ethic and a positive attitude. To my hundreds of young students who have stood in awe as I tell the story of the *Titanic*. To Robin Lowery for encouraging me to share my passion with my students. To all the teachers and parents and historians who continue to teach the story of the *Titanic* and help ensure that her memory lives on.

ABOUT THE AUTHOR

 **Mary Montero** is an author, a teacher, an avid *Titanic* enthusiast, and the entrepreneur behind the teacher's resource site, Teaching with a Mountain View. After becoming captivated by the story of *Titanic* at the age of eight, she made it her mission to pass on the *Titanic*'s legacy to her own students. She created an experience-based class on the *Titanic*, attends *Titanic* dinners at the Molly Brown House, hosts an annual commemorative *Titanic* tea with her family, and is a member of the Titanic Historical Society. She is the author of *Voices of the* Titanic.

CPSIA information can be obtained
at www.ICGtesting.com
Printed in the USA
JSHW041703230921
18798JS00003B/13